M

BY

MARY WAR

ISBN: 9781099467417

DEDICATION

Dedicated to my Mom: Thank you for picking me up when I needed to be picked up and for letting me pick myself up when you knew I could do it on my own.
To my daughter Roxanne: Thank you for being a shining beautiful light with the purest wisdom of your heart.
To all my kids Roxanne, Jacob, Daniel and Annarose, you are my heart.
And to my sister Angela whose strength and pure genuine generosity inspires me.

And to all of my family, friends and readers of this book, may your lives be joyous and blessed.

CONTENTS

Acknowledgments i

1 Thankful 3

2 Optimistic 5

3 Happy 8

4 Depressed / Sad 10

5 Fear / Addiction 17

6 Love 19

7 Silly 21

8 Nostalgic 26

9 Wishful / Hopeful 28

10 Patriotic 30

11 Festive 31

12 Angry 32

13 Deep Thoughts 35

14 Greif 40

15 Spiritual 45

ACKNOWLEDGMENTS

With great pain and happiness in our lives, I acknowledge the experiences that these poems have come to be written. It's taken years to put together. I read them to friends, family and co workers who encouraged me to compile them. I am privileged to bring this poem compilation of moods that we go through in life.

To my children: Roxanne Lay, Jacob Hurst, Daniel Hurst, Annarose Hurst, my son and daughter in laws Michael Millberg, Mandy Hurst and Bianca Hurst thank you for inspiring me to be better everyday. To my sister Angela Guerra, you are such an amazing inspiration of hope, ambition and perseverance.

To my mom- Mary Ann Bolognia-Ross thank you for your supporting advise to "get these poems printed out!".

To my boyfriend Corey James Smith, thank you for encouraging and inspiring me to set aside my fear and finish this book, work to achieve our mutual goals and for playing guitar for me while I work on this book.

To my best friend Michelle Winter, thank you for being so supportive and for being just absolutely fabulous.

To my very good friends and family: Louis Landrau, Melissa and Greg Vaccariello, Jasmin and Carl Millberg, Sam and Sue Guerra, Elena and Todd Arms, Fred Bolognia, David Guerra (fellow poet and writer), Tracy Cox-Osterhaut, Lynn Guerra, Amanda Everson, Tina Jansen, Betty Jo and Christopher Hutter, Laura Burd, Libbie Hamrick, Greg Smith, Tony Hutter, Adam Piwowar, Neeta Persaud, Lisa Zabaglo, Christina Balleweg, my aunts Cathy and Toni, Jacob Winter, Nancy Shoesmith, Patty Grubbs, Rick Minch, Joseph Boudreaux, Paula Lee, Genie Walker, Chelsea Becht, Noah Begin, Jennifer Benedict, my coworkers at the county and all the Alcala, Guerra, Bolognia, Colletti, Anderson, Hutter, Millberg and Smith family members, thank you for listening to me run these poems by you no matter what "mood" you are in and for your loving support throughout my life.

In memoriam of the beautiful loved ones who have gone before me, but left their loving inspiration, to remain forever in my heart, Casey Estes, Robert Guerra, Louise and Samuel Guerra, Rosemary Bolognia, Betty Crook, David Ross, Meryl Winter, Sue and Bob Anderson, Jeanna Howard, Jessica Irwin, David Grubbs, Allen Mathew and Kyle Purcell.

Tunescrybe logo by Josh Paskavan of B & C Printing.
Cover photos by,
Elena and Todd Arms of Pahrump Photography and Maria Guerra.

"The end is like the beginning and the beginning is like the end.
Moments in between there were times to be straight and times to bend.
These poems full of moments in someone's life.
Moments of joy and moments that cut you like a knife." ~ Mary War

1
THANKFUL

Eyes Open

Eyes open.
Thank you for this day.
Enter the burn in my stomach, enter the pain in my brain.
Still, thank you for this day.
Coffee calms my head and puts my stomach at bay.
Thank you for this day.
Face the day with a smile.
Face the day, walk this mile.
One mile will turn into two.
Will I wear the color blue?
It doesn't matter what color I wear.
As long as I treat the world with care.
I will wear a smile,
And a dress......

Thankful

Looking up at the clear sky.
Hoping we don't have to ask why.
Looking up at the stars and the moonlight above.
Knowing we are filled with love.
Listen to the rustling trees.
Getting down on my knees.
Thankful for this day.
I fold my hands and pray.

Thank you for the Music

I lay here and listen to you play guitar as I fall asleep.
Beautiful notes floating through the air and land in my heart so deep.
Praying for the future as I listen.
Praying for awareness and vision.
Thank you for the music so masterfully composed.
Thank you for the music, if it were a flower it would be a rose.

In the Office

In the office there are little lives coming in and coming out.

With their ups and their downs.
With their smiles and their frowns.
Do we wonder what they are thinking.?
Are they afloat or are they sinking?
Help me, help me some of them want to say.
While others say thank you, thank you.
Thank you for making a better day.

On My Mind

As the days go by and you are on my mind.
Thinking of all of your words that are so kind.
Waiting somewhat impatiently to see you again.
I'm so proud to say that you and I are friends.
You're a light and the rays from the sun and the moon.
We'll be talking again and visiting soon.
Talking and sharing of what we go through.
I want to express that I appreciate you.

The Sun

Behind the clouds the sun hides there.
Awaiting the clouds to clear to show it cares.
To brighten our days and nourish our flowers.
To lift our spirits and give us fresh tomorrows.
The sun shows us great power exists.
Start fresh each day and let your spirit lift.

2
OPTIMISTIC

Make Things Better

Truth is what I like to write.
The truth of my view and my own sight.
Sometimes we feel truths aren't the same.
This doesn't mean anyone is to blame.
If the same truth you do not see,
What do you see differently?
Is my view from far too close?
Is your view midway yet still with love?
Would you mind if we sit together?
See each others truths and make things better.

Collection of Words

Isn't it funny how a collection of words can remind you of times that
have gone by?
Isn't it funny how a collection of words can make you laugh or make
you cry?
Words that make you think, words that make you ponder.
Words that make you happy for just a little longer.
Words that pierce you, words that cut.
Words that make you sick deep inside your gut.
Painful inspiration rises up with good vibration.
Those words go inside your brain helping you release the pain.
Feeling good is a foreign feeling.
Sometimes it can leave you reeling.
As time goes by the words come out.
Sometimes they can make me shout.
Sometimes it's best if my moods going awry.
I crack a joke instead of cry.

Seeing the Unseen

Seeing the unseen rising from my head.
Connecting thoughts into musical thread.
Darkness and joy coming out of me in a tune.
Art becoming real very soon.
Will you hear what I'm saying?
As I let you inside my head as I'm playing?
Lost in my thoughts sometimes my brain becomes hazy.
Giving music to the world keeps me from going crazy.
Hear it, sing it, listen to me playing.
Hear it, sing it, music is me praying.
Take a walk with me.
I'll let you in come and see.
You've seen my blood, sweat and tears.
The music expresses my love and my fears.

Kind

Kind is not just a type of thing.
Not just what kind of eggs do you want or
what kind of shoes do you flaunt.

Kind is something you can give.
Kind is something you can live.

Kind is smiling at someone sad.
Hoping it will turn them glad.
Kind is hugging dad and mom.
Kind is taking a friend along.
Kind is sharing half your lunch, for someone in a bit of a crunch.
Can you think of kind things to do?
To make someone happy that's feeling blue.

Kind is something we can share to show others that we care.

Kind is something you can give.
Kind is something you can live.

Be kind everyday... and smile.

Look Around

Look around and find beauty. Look around and find sad.
Find the beauty and it's not so bad.
Beauty is everywhere.
If you look…and if you care.

Find a solution for strife.
Find a solution in life.
Troubles then aren't as bad.
They still might make you sad.

If a rain cloud follows your heart full of sorrow.
Let the rain wash it away for a fresh start tomorrow.

Look at This Life We Lead

Look at this life we lead.
We cry, we laugh, we bleed.
We cry when we are happy, we cry when we have pain.
Sometimes feeling better underneath the rain.
We laugh at jokes when we are happy.
Humor makes us laugh, even when we are feeling crappy.
We bleed for real from a scrape or cut.
We bleed emotionally and feel it in our gut.
Look at this life we lead.
Cherish the happy, it's what we need.

3
HAPPY

Home (Mine was California)

You go to a place I used to call home, California.
Know you are never alone.
California.
The friends you have are close and dear.
California.
The friends and family that live far are still near.
California.
You all stick together out there.
California.
Know those of us here still care.
California.
You all stay safe and have a ball.
California.
We are a short drive away or a call..
California.
If you must be reckless just be safe too.
California.
May cheer, love and good fortune stay with you.
In California.

Home (Variation)

You go to a place I used to call home.
Know you are never alone.
The friends you have are close and dear.
The friends and family that live far are still near.
You all stick together out there.
Know those of us here still care.
You all stay safe and have a ball.
We are a short drive away or a call..
If you must be reckless just be safe too.
May cheer, love and good fortune stay with you.

8

Guitar

Hearing the guitar gives my soul a lift.
Guitar notes are a musical gift.
It reaches my soul, sometimes I shiver.
It pulls the toxic from my liver.

I invite it in.

"Cleanse me music, fill my soul!"
It does both, I feel more whole.

So Much Love in My Heart for You

I have so much love in my heart for you.
It's true.
I'm filled with pride and admiration.
You have so much determination.
You always do what is right.
You don't take the easy flight.
I love you always you are my best friend.
I trust you and respect you and this will never end.
Thank you for your friendship, I know that you care.
You make me laugh, genuinely rare.
So much love in my heart for you.
It's true.

4
DEPRESSED/ SAD

Broken Stone

In my heart is a broken stone.
Is that why I feel alone?
Family can't see the emptiness in my soul.
Without them I can't feel whole.
As long as they don't want to see.
What is the point of me?
Would it matter if I wasn't here?
Maybe not is what I fear.
I dig deep in my heart and know I still care.
Do I abandon what I love? Will they even be aware?
If I was absent from their lives,
would they feel an empty space inside?
Ignore my efforts is what they do.
Are they casting me aside until I'm through?
"I love you" is what I would say to them.
Please remember that I tried to mend.
I'm sorry if I wasn't there.
It's not because I didn't care.
Money is what rules the land.
I never have a lot on hand.
If you want to find me.
Close your eyes and think and see.
A call or a text to the number I have.
To hear from you I would certainly be glad.

Clinical Depression

Clinical Depression,
by itself, its own obsession.
Telling me to stay down from within.
I wonder how long it's been.
Hard to rise up from the couch.
Just watch TV and be a slouch.
Stay in bed.
Soak up dread.
Energy is a commodity I don't have in stock.
The minutes speeding up the clock.
Everyday feels like the first step up the staircase.
I feel like I'm standing in the same place.
Troubled mind, troubled soul.
When I ask will I feel whole?

Silence

Why do I want to burst into tears?
Why has fear chased after me all these years?
It's like a tornado in my heart spinning me around.
Only I'm silent and stuck, afraid to make a sound.
Silence is loud, but you cannot hear it.
Silence is loud, I just fear it.
I'm afraid of the quiet in the deep, dark night.
I prepare myself to battle it with light.

See It

See it right in front of us pretending we don't feel a thing.
Watch it break and build back up just repeat it all the same.
How can we break the cycle when it's all we know that's real.
The pain part of normal, how do we change how we feel?
Barely strong enough to wake up, weak enough to sleep.
Hiding my reality, the secrets that I keep.

Amazing Mess

Life is an amazing mess.
Times filled with laughter, tears, love and stress.
In an instant life can change.
A death, a life, so many things we have to rearrange.
I find it hard to just cherish the good times.
I find it hard to stay in the lines.
Love is an amazing mess.
Beautiful and horrifying, sometimes the definition of stress.
The heart is cruel, fragile and weak.
It seems simple….its only love we seek.
Why do I want to love anyway.
When you loose it life seems to decay..
Its like mutilating your own soul.
Every time you loose it you are further from whole.

Sadness Fills Me, Get Up

Sadness fills me, get up, get up.
It's dark in this room full of light.
I'm nauseas.
Get up.
My heart aches from piercing word after word.
Do I matter? Will I ever be heard?
Sadness fills me, get up, get up.
It's dark in this room full of light.
I'm dizzy.
Get up.

Changes

It's hard when life changes and friends go away.
It's hard when you see them to know what to say.
If I didn't care, I could just let go and say goodbye.
Sometimes I wish I didn't care so it wouldn't make me cry.

There Is No
What would it be like if I could wrap myself with you.
If you wanted this, if you needed this, if you felt the same for me.
I imagine it would be lovely.
It's only something to imagine. It's not real.
Maybe my heart and soul are lying to me?
Maybe it's evil bringing this love.
What else could conjure such powerful love that brings only pain.
There is no peace.
There is no hope.
There is no love.
Acceptance is complacent.
Joy, love, hope, smiles, peace.
Existing only in small pockets for the luckiest of souls.
Even our most precious love- our children.
We would suffer for them
We would die for them.
They have no idea until they fill our shoes.
The time is past.
Let all your love pass through time and space and become one with the energy of the universe.
And may the luckiest and most deserving receive it without the pain the rest of us feel when it's lost.
I lie to myself as your arms wrap around me.
Wanting this moment to last longer if not forever.
I am dammed.
Dammed to remember this beautiful moment as a time when my heart was tragically broken and burned.
I am but a stone in the long walk down a path.
I am not this destination.
My fear is that I will remain a stone.
Why can't I feel as a stone.
A stone is stronger than a heart.
A stone would take more force to break apart.
If I were a stone I would be stronger if I were alone.
The anxiety within the center of my being is never gone.
At least not for very long.
I am loved only by those who cannot embrace me.
I am walking the earth completely free.
Free to suffer my silent pain.
Free to let tears mix with rain.

Spilling

Spilling out on the page.
All my feelings, all my rage.
Pain burrowed deeply in my soul.
Try to set it free to feel whole.
Without the pain will I feel complete?
Do I need it there for my heart to beat?
How do I keep a bit and let it go?
How do I hold on to some? How will I know?
Know a bit is there of a mistake.
So a different path now I can take.
Know a bit is there of joy that's lost.
For those fond memories have no cost.
Spilling out on the page.
This pain no longer keeps me caged.

Turn

Turn your face away from me as if I'm not even there.
This is why I think you don't care.
You tell me that you love me. Then you turn away.
I wish you would notice- I'm not ok.
Maybe I spend too much time worrying about you.
Just know this worry is a prayer for us too.

Heavy Sorrow

Heavy sorrow invades my mind.
I know others feel sorrow of the same kind.
The world can be a cruel place.
It's hard to believe beauty occupies the same space.

How

When my spirit is in the pits of hell.
Suffering, I can't believe how far I fell.
With no idea how to free myself from the flaming rope.
With no idea how I will cope.

Path of Sorrow

Destined to walk this path of sorrow and despair.
Destined to inhale sorrow with every breath of air.
Happiness has left my heart.
A misunderstanding has torn us apart.
I'm scared the pain will sear my soul.
Without my friend I am not whole.
Fear is taking over and paralyzing my ambition.
I can't eat or drink, I'm losing my cognition.
I'm writing down what I am feeling.
Hoping it will help with healing.
It's too soon to smile it's too soon to wake.
Maybe there's a pill to take.
The pill is a trap, so I won't take it.
My heart is no stranger to pain, I guess I'll make it.
It would just be nice to smile again.
It's just hard because I don't know when.

It's a Shame

I'm your friend but you're not mine.
You put our friendship at the back of the line.
You let someone else decide who you could befriend.
Your betrayal is forgiven as my heart mends.
The life I live today I love.
God must have blessed me from above.
It's just a shame you're not here to see.
The wonderful things God has brought to me.

Chasing a Dream

What kind of life have I made.
Chasing this dream of happiness.
Chasing a dream - that laughs in my face as I fight to keep it afloat.
Dreams...dreams... Stay with me.
You're heavy.
I'm pulling and lifting you up to my heart.
You are fighting me.
Why are you so heavy?
Do you not want to be in this dream?
Happiness is all I seek.
The path I have chosen takes my will.
It's heavy.
The burden of love is a weary and heavy one.
Is this real?
Am I caught in a spiral of lies that is draining my soul and stealing my love.
What kind of life have I made.
Chasing this dream of happiness.
Chasing a dream - that laughs in my face as I fight to keep it afloat.
Dreams...dreams... Stay with me.

Wide Awake

Wide awake all I feel is pain in my head, neck, heart and soul.
Am I a broken person? Will I ever be whole?
Walk around with circling anxiety.
Like a ball and chain surrounding me.
As you think you've discovered your goals and dreams.
Things may not be as they seem.
Sometimes sitting in my own skin is a nightmare.
Wishing for just a hug to show me some care.
Aware this feeling is temporary.
They're just draining and make me weary.
Dig deep to find a bit more strength.
Dig deep to go the extra length.
Look for the ray of light.
Keep going stay in the fight.

5
FEAR / ADDICTION

Tick, Tick, Tick

Tick, tick, tick.
Ding, ding, ding.
Put your money in and watch it go.
Pay for the chandelier and the big Vegas shows.
Do you think they built this town on sand alone?
It's your blood, sweat and broken back.
It puts this town on the map.
If it's a couple of bucks for fun you're fine.
But if you crave it it's a matter of time.
You'll lie and you'll spend.
You'll hurt and need to mend.
Hopefully your dollar comes back.
But if you keep chasing it you've lost your knack.

Middle of the Night

In the middle of the night, I get ill.
To help this there is no pill.
Restless thoughts race through my brain.
Cluster clouds, pouring rain.
I'm sick. It's the middle of the night.
It's so dark. Panic and fear shine bright.
Searing pain runs through my gut.
Lying fetal in a depressive rut.
Panic I may not get up to live.
I want it though to live and give.
Fall asleep again in the middle of the night.
Pray I wake up tomorrow to fight the good fight.

Earthquake of '94

I see an earthquake on the screen and I remember the fear.
Like it was yesterday when it was here.
I remember the crashes, explosions and screams.
I remember the months following and the horrible dreams.
The day the house, ground and earth shook.
We were all scared to look.
At the damage and wreckage of that 7 something quake.
I remember the day as we all came to wake.
It was early morning and still dark outside.
As the Earth shook and things began to collide.

The Drink

Is the drink in front of you the most important thing in life?
Is it more important than your kids, husband or wife?
Does it give you all that you need?
Do you worship it with a creed?

What does it have that you give up your future?
Inside the bottle, can or pill is only torture.
Can you love nothing else except the drink in your hand?
When you were a kid, I know this wasn't your plan.

Has our life been a lie? A waiting room in which you leave to seek the destruction of your soul. Your heart is not made of coal.

The drinking and the drugs may help you escape your fears and demons temporarily.
Only to find you wake with more demons and fears that make your heart more weary.
You have to know that alcohol and drugs will destroy you.
Until you are dead their work is not through.
You will feel worse than the pain that brought you to them in the beginning.
I know the transition is hard and you are holding on by a string.
If you can find just a hint of the love and hope your family and friends hold on to.
Be strong, hold on, I believe you will pull through.

6
LOVE

We Love <3

Life is so busy there are so many we love.
Life is so busy, we look to God above.

Please let them know we love them.
Please let them know we care.

Let them know they are in our hearts.
And, our connection is still there.
So many of our loved ones are in heaven by your side.
Please let them know they are in our hearts and their spirit is still alive.
We shall never forget the love they gave when they could hold our hands and pray.
We shall never forget the love they gave, it will be in our hearts everyday.

Hope

A story of hope, strength and love can inspire your soul.
Sharing with others can make you whole.
Music can fill your heart with hope and love.
Imagine the grace of a soaring dove.
Share with others peace, hope and strength and you will become stronger.
Faith and life will last longer.
Accept love and care with genuine grace.
Let kindness fill our air and our space.

As you touch me

Loosing myself as you touch me.
Captured and captivated, I've never felt so free.
Through my spine, I purr as if I was kitten.
My arms wrapped around you, I'm smitten.

This Soul

A fragile soul with such a rough exterior.
This soul is not inferior.
Kicking, biting, scratching at everything that comes near.
Shut off to anything that could get in from fear.
Vulnerable to the softness inside.
Fear and strength within may collide.
Expose it and face it and tear down the wall.
Strength and love will answer the call.

7
SILLY

Bob's Your Uncle

Bob's your uncle but he's my dad.
The greatest gift he ever had.
Was me his daughter and my sister too.
He went and died and now we're blue.

Planet of Dork

I come from the planet of Dork.
For dinner we eat rice and pork.
None of our dogs have any fleas.
But all of our dogs eat green peas.
We live in purple houses with blue trees outside.
We eat fresh veggies but all of our fruit is fried.

Shilby O'Gill

Shilby O'Gill it's a song about will.
Will you sit with me by the fire.
Sit with me and admire.
My painting of birds,
O haven't you heard.
Shilby O'Gill is a painter.
Shilby O'Gill it's a song about will.
Oh will you come eat some bacon.
It's breakfast time and you should be a wakin'.
Shilby O'Gill it's a song about will.
Oh will you play the fiddle.
I'll play the guitar, he can play bass and you can stand in the middle.
Shilby O'Gill it's a song about will.
The drummer got drunk and said fuck it.
Get one eyed Ed out of his bed and he can drum on a bucket.

Weirdest Things

The weirdest things run through my head.
Even when I'm alone laying in my bed.
I would say I have to agree even with myself and me.
Though I wonder what might be true.
I always know the sky is blue.
If you could see inside my brain.
It would mean you were traveling on a cellular train.

Moonshine and Monkeys

Moonshine and monkeys are two of my favorite things.
I drink that moonshine and my monkey has wings.
I think that moonshine may be too strong.
I've been drinking this for far too long.
When monkeys fly, and turtles cry.
I've got to ask myself why.
Why this apple pie moonshine?
Why not sophisticated wine?
Because monkeys and moonshine are two of my favorite things.
And, I know my monkey doesn't really have wings.

Little Italian Whipper Snapper

Little Italian Whipper Snapper yells at the drop of a hat.
Little Italian Whipper Snapper screams like a feral cat.
Pasta and meatballs and fresh garlic toast.
Or, roasted potatoes with garlic stuffed roast.
No matter what she makes that day, it's always so delicious.
You better eat what you put on your plate or she just may get vicious.
"Manja, Manja", she will say until you finish your food.
You eat it all till you're really full. I mean you don't want to be rude.

I'm So Silly

Around you I'm so silly.
My brain goes silly nilly.
I've been a fan for many years.
Through laughter and tears.
Music is what connects my soul.
I need music so I feel whole.
In a busy life, music takes my mind on a mini vacation.
Some days it's my only elation.

Traffic Court

Traffic Court making money for the roads.
Traffic Court, reduce the charges but you still pay loads.
Money is what rules the land.
No points on your record if you have cash in hand.
Doesn't matter if you're guilty or innocent.
Doesn't matter if you can't pay the rent.
The court will get the money, the court will make you pay.
You give them your money so you can move on with your day.
The cops and judges have families to feed.
You pay the money as your wallet bleeds.
Use my Discover to get cash back for my crime.
Charge it to get it over with so you don't have to do time.

Sometimes I'd Eat Flowers

Once I was little girl.
Living in my own little world.
Collecting rocks and squishing bugs, even if they were on the rugs.
And sometimes I'd eat flowers.

Poppy was the flower that I liked to eat the most.
One time in the backyard, I thought I saw ghost!
Turns out I was just really high, As a six year old that made me cry.
And sometimes I'd eat flowers.

Over Goodbye er'

Do you ever keep talking on the phone,
Or say goodbye to long?
Do you ever give extra hugs,
Or keep saying just this one more song?
Do you always walk your family out,
And keep waving till they're gone?
Do you give 14 hugs and make goodbyes last for far too long?

You just might be an over goodbye er' like me.
Just sending love over and over till your guests are free.
When they leave after a visit doesn't mean they don't love you.
Just means that for now your visit is just through.
Over goodbye er'
Over goodbye er'
It's ok to let them go home.
Over goodbye er'
Over goodbye er'
Don't be afraid to be alone.

A Collection of Park Poems

I was sitting on a bench in the park.
A little gloomy but not dark.
I saw a bird flying.
It seemed as if it was crying.
It appeared to be a lark.

I was running through the park with a kite.
It started taking flight.
I was running out of string.
I pulled on that thing.
It gave me a bit of a fright.

I was in the park eating chips.
I was getting salt on my lips.
On the grass, I took a walk.
Hearing the chirping birds having their talk.
So I sat on the grass and ate grapes.
Thinking…..I need new drapes.

I was in the park on the swing.
I almost fell off that thing.
I'm looking up at the sky so blue.
Oh dear I just lost my shoe.

8
NOSTALGIC

Babysitter

Back when I was 7 years of age.
At times things would cause me some rage.
I wanted to tell my mom I missed my dad
But my mom was out and a babysitter we had.
I wanted to call and ask my mom if my dad could come get us.
But the babysitter said I would have to ask my mom, she didn't have the number so she couldn't let us.
I said to her, "I'll call information for the number".
When they couldn't help me it was a bummer.
The babysitter said, "I told you so".
So then she just had to go.
Let her think everything is fine.
Little did she know the plan was mine.
I called my dad, he said "you're not alone".
I had to get her out so my dad would come home.
A plan was devised no time did it take.
Lucky for me more for her was at stake.
I told my little sis to follow my lead.
I was about to embark on a mischievous deed.
I'll sneak out and ring the door bell.
She'll come to the door thinking everything's well.
She fell for it! I said a man was asking for my mom outside.
She went out to look, I locked her out, and she cried.
I remember feeling bad.
But if I let her in I won't see my dad.
She ended up walking home.
After that we were all alone.
I called my dad back and said "the babysitter's gone."
"Now get over here, it won't take long."

Something Special

Something special in the air.
Something special if you care.
Something special are the trees.
Something special are the bees.
Something special is the sounds of the birds.
Special is the sounds of our loved ones words.

Rabbit Hole

I climbed out of a rabbit hole one day with clarity to start living.
Aware of everything and what I could be giving.
I could remember the past as if it were a dream.
It wasn't as real a memory as it should seem.
How is it that such fog can be present or here.
How is it that my memories are not clear.
I felt as if through my journey I was not aware.
However feeling as if through my journey though I did care.
Memories faint and precious intact.
My life now feels on track.

Grandma

I think about the day I saw my grandma, I hadn't seen her for a while.
I think about the day I saw my grandma, I had driven many miles.
As I gave her a hug my eyes filled with tears.
She was always so caring, all of her years.
She said "Meja why are you crying?"
I said "I miss you grandma." The trip was trying.
Her health was getting worse, to loose her I feared.
She said to me" But, Meja I'm right here."

9
WISHFUL/HOPEFUL

Aliens

Aliens among us, clouding our minds.
Aliens among us from worlds of all kinds.
Stuck in my protected cocoon,
Fishing from my own lagoon.
I hear the alien say,"I'm alone,
Can I stay and make this my home?"
In my heart I want us all to get along.
We could move freely between worlds in harmonic song.
I wish it was that simple to just let you in.
I wish it was that simple for all of us to win.

Days

Days we have not seen yet, shall be better. Pay mind to caring for others.
Let's treat others like sisters and brothers.
Protect our future days with love we build.
If you knew now what you knew then, would good be what you willed?
Cherish the days of this journey we take.
Cherish the memories we have yet to make.

I See

I see a beautiful sunset.
I let go of regret.
I see a clear night, rich with stars in the sky.
I just enjoy it and don't ask why.
I feel a soft breeze on my face.
I enjoy being in a safe place.
I hear two birds chirping out the window.
Do they feel love and just know.
I see a painting of an English castle.
I dream of visiting there without thinking of the hassle.

Far and Here

As an eclipse happens up in space very far away,
Down here on Earth we are having a regular day.
Most of us only imagine space from a dream.
In the morning I make coffee adding sugar and cream.
In the movies space doesn't seem so far.
I drive to work slowly in my car.
The planets in orbit in the solar system.
I arrive at work with hope and vision.

My Shadow

My shadow is a princess.
My shadow doesn't settle for less.
My shadow can only live through me.
My shadow cannot see what I see.
My shadow doesn't know how hard things are in life.
My shadow doesn't feel the strife.
My shadow is that of the innocence I once knew.
When inside my heart hopes and dreams grew.

10
PATRIOTIC

America The Great

America the great. America the free.
We can all make this be.
Pray for politicians to help America succeed.
Pray for politicians to inspire and lead.
America does not need chaos, turmoil and greed.
In this wonderful country we need success.
We need to respect each other and be angry less.

Support

I support the President. Whoever that may be.
I support America, home of the brave and the land of the free.
I support America, tried and true.
I support the land of the red, white and blue.
I respect your opinion even if I don't agree.
I just ask that you respect me too, and do the same for me.

Peaceful Friendly America

Think about a peaceful friendly America.
Think about how much we could get done.
If we spent less time on conflict and anger,
This country would be in a lot less danger.
The strongest country in the world, divided will put us behind.
It boggles and confuses my mind.
America the great, America the free.
We must work together, please see.
We give our freedom away.
The price we will pay.
The price we are paying.
Please hear what I'm saying.
Think about a peaceful friendly America.

11
FESTIVE

Under the Tree

Under the tree are the presents you give, expressed with love.
As you share time together blessed by God above.
It doesn't matter what the gift.
You just hope the receivers heart will lift.
Thank you for being a part of my life and days.
Gifts help us thank and appreciate each other in so many ways.

Christmas at Work

I'm really lucky to work with a great bunch.
It's really nice when we go to lunch.
This season I bring you a Christmas thought.
Some made and some bought.
The last couple of years have been trying.
If I said otherwise, I'd be lying.
Thank you for being so thoughtful and caring.
Thank you for listening when I'm sharing.
Best wishes for the next year.
And hopes for fantastic Christmas cheer.

To my Team

This poem I wrote and rolled it up.
You found it in your Christmas cup.
Christmas is the time of year.
To come to work with love and cheer.
Time we spend together is appreciated.
My joy for work has not faded.
Throughout the year we celebrate.
Special occasions that are great.
It's nice for us to be together.
Throughout the year, throughout the weather.
This team is great, I love you all.
In winter, summer, spring and fall.

12
ANGRY

Jealousy

Jealousy is a toxic drink.
It's like poison, and you cannot think.
If you drink from it your thoughts will scew.
Unhealthy anger will make you sad and blue.
Don't let jealousy take over and present.
If its control you seek, it's your lament.
Leave harsh thoughts behind.
Jealousy can make you blind.
Jealousy hides love and happiness inside.
Angry thoughts in your brain collide.
Anarchy within your soul.
Your body will weaken as it takes its toll.

Every time

Every time I think of you, my heart fills with vengeful pain.
I want to forgive, so I don't live in vein.
You are callous and evil and full of yourself.
You made my life a hell.
You poison the hearts of the people I love. Just so they think you're
swell.
You don't even know me.
So you don't even care.
One day you will meet your maker, don't think he's unaware!
You kid yourself and others into thinking that you are good.
You should admit the pain you've caused. Do you think you ever
could?

Fool

Lash out and act like a fool.
Nothing about your behavior is cool.
You dig yourself deeper into your own egotistical hole.
Only one sided arrogance in your cereal bowl.
Eat your words, and taste your hate.
Your refusal to look outside yourself will deal your fate.
All the hate you eat up everyday.
Is a meal ticket you don't want to pay.
If you opened your eyes and only knew.
Crow is the best meal for you.
Eat it every meal until you see the wrong you do.
Only then will your suffering be through.
Delusional lies you make up in your head.
You've been a bad friend, this had to be said.
If you were a good friend others would stand by you.
Thats a fairy tale for you now, you know that too.
Only you can change your fate.
Can you save yourself from your inner hate?

Crazy Girl

Crazy girl equals insecure.
The opposite of demure.
Sick and twisted, false reality.
Your behavior leads to relationships fatality.
One of your flaws is extreme arrogance.
The things you say don't make sense.
You think you're cool to throw out threats.
It's you that will lose all your bets.
Yell at him. Yell at me.
Yell at everyone you see.
See you next Tuesday little girl.
You're acting like a parasite in this world.
You need help, you know you do.
Until you find it, this conversation is through.
Fuck off is what you say.
It's you that will fuck off today.

You Lied

You lied to take my money.
You lied to trick my heart.

You are a thief.
You should answer for what you've done.
Liar, liar, thief.

Lying about what you stole.
You have an empty soul.
Eating you up inside, all of your lies.
Let me move on and quit your lying cries.

13
DEEP THOUGHTS

Will

Does the human spirit need a reality check?
Why do we want to hit the deck?
Is that why we seek that in which instills fear from the pit of our stomach?
Letting it radiate through us to exit with a plan of survival and resolve.
Is it so our survival skills will evolve?

Full Circle

These times I thought were in the past.
Aware I was not, that time past, so fast.
Surreal I feel, as I am here.
My head is cloudy. My brain is clear.

Full circle, the journey was then, the journey is now.

It's already started but its just begun.
Plant your feet it's time to run.
Don't run too fast, and watch your stride.
The journey is here, enjoy the ride.
It's up, it's down.
There are paths all around.

All different, all good.
You won't know…it's full circle, it's fate, it's God, it's full circle.
The path to the beginning.

It's up, it's down. The paths twist, turn and part.
Will they lead you back to where you start?

Shopping

If you're shopping at a store and you see someone confused.

Do you ask what they are looking for or ask if they are ok?
Or
Do you blindly go about your shopping and be on your way?

Time

Time is a funny thing.
I can think of another time.
Close my eyes as if I'm there.
Look at a tree- it's 20 years ago.
It's not.
Appreciate today- to myself I say.
Memories of another time- still with me - to always be.
There for me to close my eyes.
To be there, briefly.
To smile.
To Laugh.
To cry.

Laws of Suppression

There wouldn't be laws of suppression if we could all get along.
Temptation governs the weak.
Resist.
Resist.
It may seem bleak.
Easy and evil start with the same letter.
Easy doesn't always make it better.
Do it right and do it well.
Bad things sit stagnate and start to smell.

Ask and Tell Myself

What is it that we need in our lives?
What is it that we need to survive?

We need air to breathe.
We need water to drink.
We need food to eat.
We need shelter to protect us.

We need these things just to survive our lives.
With this thought, what does your heart, soul and mind need for
our lives?

We need to feel love-
so our hearts will be full of happiness and joy.
Don't we?
Sometimes it hurts to feel love, when someone we love is hurting
or angry.

Life and love are all of this.
Happiness, sadness, anger, excitement, fear, worry, joy, pain,
and pleasure.

Within our hearts and minds we seek the good feeling, the joy.
We endure the other unpleasant feelings for the sake of the good.
Achieving love and happiness
is a journey very different for everyone.
Full of all the feelings we have.
Sharing good and bad feelings with others we love makes the
journey good.
Sometimes we forget the goal- happiness, peace and love.

Remember- resentment,
anger and destruction are a waste of our life.

We are going to feel hurt and sadness, but to remain angry,
hold resentment,
or be destructive puts heavy weight on our hearts
and suppresses the happiness in our minds.

We can be free of bad feelings by forgiving.
We don't have to forget or be naive to evil.
But let it go
and pray for the wickedness to stop and for compassion
and supportiveness to spread.

Life and Love are all of this.
May your journey be joyous.

Worlds Embrace

I try to fill the world around me with peace and love.
Couldn't we all embrace our world with peace and love?
Wouldn't then our lives be full of joy?

Strive for greatness over glory.
Be kind and courteous to others.
Work hard.
Recycle to protect our Earth's resources.
Appreciate our rewards.
Teach our children love and responsibility.
Learn and expand our knowledge.
Protect each other.

Everyone matters.
We must care.

With this and goodness, on any scale, we can all make a difference
and achieve greatness in our world.

Make a difference.
Make someone smile.
Share with our world the goodness, love and kindness.

We all are the world.
We are peace and love.
Happiness, strength and love are up to all of us.

Pray and send wishes and hopes of happiness and goodness to all in
our world.
And, may God bless the brave souls who strive to protect it.

14
GRIEF

I Will Remember

No longer here to say, "How are you". No longer here to talk.
No longer here to give us a hug. No longer here to take a walk.
Leaving us with the question "Why?"
To grieve and hurt and cry.
I will remember your smile, and sass and strengths.
I will remember you helped others and went to great lengths.
I will remember the wild times that we had.
I will remember to be grateful and glad.
Glad in our lives we were friends with each other.
Glad I knew the love you had as a mother.
Thank you for being my friend.
Know I love you to the end.
I will remember you for as long as I live.
Love to your family I'll always give.
I send peaceful wishes to you in heaven above.
I send prayers to you with all my love.

My friend, so sassy, sweet, kind, strong and dear.
May you receive messages of love loud and clear.

Rest in peace, my friend.

Pain

Pain of love, pain of loss.
Pain you hope to never come across.
It changes you the pain so deep.
Sometimes questioning the faith of a leap.
Lovely is joy when you feel it inside.
Pain and joy, a roller coaster ride.

Fear

What do I do here?
I'm scared and full of fear.
I love you so much and I'm full of fear.
I can't stand the pain, I want you near.
I used to like the the term keep moving forward.
I don't now because I'm moving toward.
Toward a life that's full of fear.
Toward a life where you aren't here.

One Year Ago Today

One year ago today you were taken away.
One year ago today all of our lives changed.
Our love, son, uncle, brother, and best friend.
The memories of you will never end.
Our lives are better because we had the privilege of loving you.
I know you loved us all too.
I hope you know you are always in my heart.
Even though now we are worlds apart.
Your life mattered and impacted us all.
One year ago today though you answered Gods call.
We know you are safe in the heavens above.
And you know now the greatest of Gods love.
When I'm sad and missing you so much.
That's when I hear the birds and know we are still in touch.
The love we all have for you will connect us forever.
We will carry your strength with us in every endeavor.
One year ago today our lives all changed.
One year ago today we had to face life being rearranged.
It's a hard road without you here.
Holding on to your strength will help us face the fear.
Dear One, Please Rest In Peace and Love.
Please Watch over us with God from above.

It's Been a Week

Now it's been a week.
Life still dreary, sad and bleak.
How can this be happening?
Do you have your angel wings?
I'm sure yo do, you are so loved.
I believe you're soaring with God above.
I'm holding on to every word, keeping you in my heart.
I'm thinking of your touch, wishing we never had to part.

Every Day/ Everything

Every day coffee, every day lunch.
Every day dinner, I miss you so much.

How can I enjoy anything again without you by my side.
My best friend I wish you were alive.
How can I live without you, can this pain be real.
How can I breathe another minute, it's just you I want to feel.
I want you back, I feel like I may die.
I want you back, the pain brings my never-ending cry.

Everything in life was we.
Everyday in life was you and me.
Together we conquered everyday.
Together it was you and me all the way.
How do I do this without you here.
How do I ever hold on to any cheer.
You are my heart. You were my days.
You were my nights. My always.

You

You were so beautiful inside.
From sorrow you couldn't always hide.
You were so precious and true.
I love you.
Now that you have gone away,
Home to the Lord I have to say.
I wish I could understand.
I just want to hold your hand.
I'll miss you every minute.
My life was blessed because you were in it.

Tonight

Tonight I getting bed without you by my side.
I wish I could turn back time so we could go somewhere and hide.
I wish upon a star.
For your spirit to not be far.
I miss you more than words can say.
I pray for strength to rise each day.

Crushed

I feel I'm being crushed inside.
Wishing you had not died.
I just want to scream.
Wake me from this horrible dream.

I Hope

I'm thankful for the love we shared.
I hope to God you were aware.
Your life was beautiful and dear.
I hope from heaven you can hear.
Hear my love transcending earth.
To reach your heart and know your worth.

Without You

Without you my silliness will be gone for a while.
Until after I walk this mile.
This mile of sorrow and lonely nights.
Missing you so bad from our love to our fights.
I'm shaking from ache, my head throbbing from pain.
I feel like my soul is spiraling down a drain.

Grace

I will always adore your beautiful soul, love and face.
I pray my grief transforms to you in grace.
Grace and peace for your beautiful soul.
Grace and peace for your heart to be whole.
You were a blessing and showed me love dear and true.
A love and a friendship that just always grew.
May God grant you the most joyous and tranquil heavenly sleep.
May you know your love with me I will always keep.

Too Few

I am so very grateful to have spent these years with you.
They may seem many, but to me they were too few.
My heart was happy through these years.
Through happiness, silliness and also tears.
I do not know if I will mend, if at all.
I'll remember your spirit to lift me when I fall.

15
SPIRITUAL

Candid/Why

Candid in our thoughts we are when anger fills our mind.
Candid in our thoughts we are when anger makes us blind.
Why can't we express love when it enters our heart?
Why can't we express love before anger tears us apart?
"Why" is the lock.
"Why" is the key.
"Why" is overwhelming, it's why we can't see.
"Why" is the key.
"Why" is the lock.
"Why" is the question of some of God's flock.
Faith is the why.
Faith is what's true.
Faith keeps us together.
Faith is the glue.

Together We Heal

I didn't look in my rearview mirror, what does that mean?
I was driving forward, all the lights were green.
Please don't stop me from personal growth.
Please accept this as my personal oath.
I wish for the sick to be well again.
I wish for my prayers to be heard in heaven.
I don't want anyone to die.
I'm always asking why.

Why can't we all move forward?

Why can't we all want more?
Not for material gain, just to be happy in our core.
Just to have a happy soul and have a happy life.
Just to help others get rid of strife.
Struggles are hard, struggles are real.
Find the strength to move forward, together we heal.

I Pray

Why is it the fog looms in my head?
Why is it I can't get out of bed?
Crazy thoughts racing in my mind.
Bewildering thoughts of their own kind.
Coffee may help the fog dissipate.
Coffee may help my mind relate.
Relate to the errands I have today.
Relate to the thoughts and words I pray.
I pray I greet my family with love.
I pray my prayers are heard by God above.
I feel God hears my prayers the fog is clearing.
I find my family kind and endearing.
Thank lord for hearing my plea.
My faith grows stronger inside of me.

ABOUT THE AUTHOR

Maria Guerra, penning her book as Mary War (the English translation of her name) was born and grew up in Simi Valley, California. She developed a love for music and the arts. She would write just as a hobby and always hoped to write stories, poems, jingles and lyrics professionally one day. She lived around and worked with musicians and bands over the years and started writing again after moving to Nevada, where she currently lives with her boyfriend and daughter. There she started working for the Nevada WIC Program and local TV station as a talk show host. She served throughout the years on festival entertainment committees, children's theater and arts council committees, and food security committees. She has emceed and hosted music festivals, produced sold out comedy/music variety shows and written songs for various bands. She has an eclectic style and especially loves live music, going to the movies and writing comedic songs and poems. She attended Great Basin College to study writing and acting to enhance her TV persona, interviewing skills and writing projects. She recently formed a writing and entertainment management and promotion company called Tune Scrybe, which she hopes to share not only her work but the work of fellow writers, artists and entertainers. She is currently working as a nutrition and lactation counselor, TV talk show host, reporter, and Band manager as well as serving on community committees, writing her poems, songs and short stories.

tunescrybe@gmail.com